A DAY AT THE GALLERY

Nia Gould

Written and edited
by Susannah Bailey

Illustrated by
Nia Gould

Designed by Barbara Ward
Cover design by John Bigwood

First published in Great Britain in 2021 by
LOM ART, an imprint of Michael O'Mara Books Limited,
9 Lion Yard, Tremadoc Road, London SW4 7NQ

W   www.mombooks.com/lom
f   Michael O'Mara Books
𝕏   @OMaraBooks
📷   @lomartbooks

A CIP catalogue record for this book is available from the British Library.

ISBN: 978-1-912785-36-0

10 9 8 7 6 5 4 3 2 1

This book was printed in January 2021 by Shenzhen Wing King Tong
Paper Products Co. Ltd., Shenzhen, Guangdong, China.

Welcome to the Gallery

A group of animals have taken a trip to the gallery to learn about modern art. There are many paintings and sculptures to see – some are bright and colourful, while others are strange and mysterious.

Each room in the gallery displays work by artists who belonged to the same 'movement'. This means their art is grouped together because they were inspired by the same things and are similar in style. You'll find out the names of artists who belonged to different movements and about their ideas.

Along the way, there are fun things to spot in each gallery. You'll find the answers at the back of the book, along with a helpful timeline and a glossary.

What are you waiting for?
Turn the page to enter the gallery ...

Light and Time

The foxes are learning all about IMPRESSIONISM. They can't wait to see paintings of waterlilies and ballet dancers.

The most famous Impressionist painters were **Claude Monet**, **Pierre-Auguste Renoir** and **Edgar Degas**.

Impressionists weren't trying to make realistic-looking copies of objects and people. They captured the **'impression'** of what something looked like to them at the **moment** they saw it.

Impressionist artists often worked **outdoors**. They painted **quickly** so they could fully catch a scene before the **light** changed.

Follow the foxes on their way to the Impressionist Gallery. Can you see ...

A fox in the water?

A picnic basket?

A black hat?

A dancer's crown?

Extra spots

A fox on his **phone**

A fox taking **notes**

A stripy **scarf**

A blue **bow tie**

A pair of **glasses**

Layers and Emotions

The kangaroos want to know about POST-IMPRESSIONISM. The artists in this movement experimented with new styles, rather than copying those who came before them.

The most famous Post-Impressionist painters were **Vincent van Gogh**, **Paul Gauguin** and **Paul Cézanne**.

Post-Impressionist painters used **vivid colours** and applied **thick layers** of paint to their canvasses.

The main painters in this movement had very different styles, but they all wanted to show **feelings** and **emotion** in their art.

Join the kangaroos as they go to the Post-Impressionist Gallery. Can you find ...

A hand of cards?

A crescent moon?

A coconut?

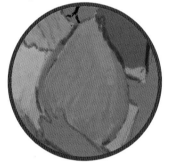

An umbrella?

Extra spots

A **purple paintbrush** in a pouch

Two **blue babies**

A piece of **paper**

A **book**

A kangaroo with a **navy pouch**

Thoughts and Feelings

The llamas are reading about EXPRESSIONISM. They're excited to see all of the swirling colours and abstract pictures in the gallery.

The most famous Expressionist artists were **Wassily Kandinsky, Edvard Munch** and **Franz Marc.**

Expressionists wanted to show their **inner thoughts** in their art. They judged art by the **feeling** it showed, rather than how it was made.

Expressionist works often feature large **brushstrokes**. The artists wanted to paint **fast** to get down all the strong **emotions** they were having at the time of painting.

Follow the llamas, who are off to the Expressionist Gallery. Can you see ...

Two prickly cacti?

A sun?

A sombrero?

A worried llama?

Extra spots

A pink **backpack**

A **baby** on a mother's back

A llama **knitting**

A **skateboard**

Three **coloured crayons**

Expressionist Gallery

Colour and Brushstrokes

The mice have arrived to learn all about FAUVISM. They've heard the painters use bright, unnatural colours in their works.

The most famous Fauvist artists were **Henri Matisse, Marc Chagall** and **André Derain.**

'**Les fauves**' is French for '**the wild beasts**'. Fauvist artists got this name because they used bold, unexpected **colours** and worked with loose, free **brushstrokes**.

Matisse was part of many different art movements. Early in his career he was a Fauvist, then later on he used Fauvist ideas in **collage**, cutting and arranging colourful **paper shapes**.

Join the mice as they travel to the Fauvist Gallery. Can you see ...

A bird?

A heart?

A piece of cheese?

A musical instrument?

Extra spots

A **mouse** reading a **leaflet**

A **baby** in a **pushchair**

A **mouse** door

A **scooter**

A **walking** stick

Fauvist Gallery

GIFT SHOP

21

Shapes and Angles

The bears want to know more about CUBISM. It is very different to any art they've seen before.

The most famous Cubist artists were **Pablo Picasso, Georges Braque** and **Marcel Duchamp**.

Cubists are known for using lots of **geometric shapes** in their paintings. The movement was called 'Cubism' because the shapes often looked like **cubes**.

Cubists liked to paint objects, landscapes or people from **different angles** in the **same** painting. They felt this was a better way of showing something, but not everyone in the art world agreed.

Follow the bears all the way to the Cubist Gallery. Can you see ...

A jar of honey?

Honey

An earring?

A square bear?

A patchwork bear?

Extra spots

A **bear** taking a **selfie**

A **bear** wearing **glasses**

A blue **scarf**

A **hair bow**

An **audio guide**

Dreams and Imagination

The cats are reading about SURREALISM. The art here feels like it's part of a different world.

The most famous Surrealist painters were **Salvador Dalí**, **René Magritte** and **Frida Kahlo**.

Surrealist artists were inspired by **dreams**. They wanted to paint all the weird things that our minds **imagine**, rather than showing reality.

Surrealist paintings contain strange **creatures** and oddly shaped **people** and **objects**. Surrealist artists put **unexpected** things next to each other in their pictures.

Join the cats as they visit the Surrealist Gallery. Can you see ...

An apple?

A fishy eye?

A red fish?

A hummingbird?

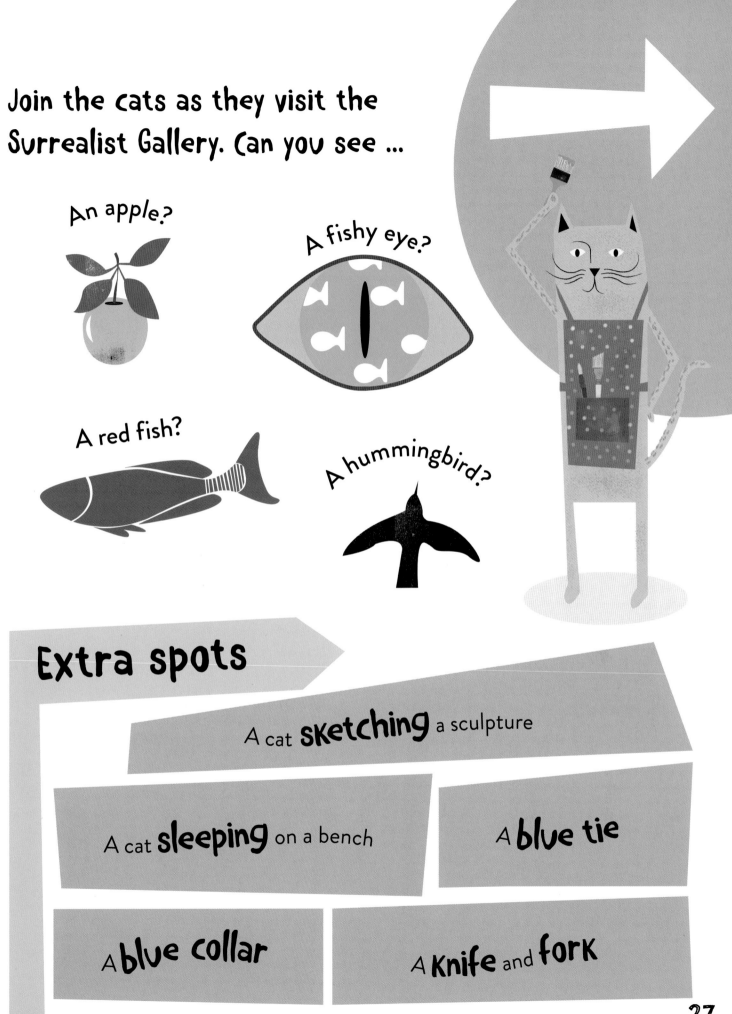

Extra spots

A cat **sketching** a sculpture

A cat **sleeping** on a bench

A **blue tie**

A **blue collar**

A **knife** and **fork**

Surrealist Gallery

Splashes and Splatters

The monkeys have come to learn about ABSTRACT EXPRESSIONISM. They love all the wild paint splatters and fun shapes.

The most famous Abstract Expressionist artists were **Jackson Pollock, Mark Rothko** and **Lee Krasner.**

Jackson Pollock is called an **'action painter'**. He put his canvasses on the floor and walked around dropping paint onto them to make his pictures. They were known as **drip paintings**.

Mark Rothko was a **'colour field'** artist. He painted large, solid **rectangles**, each in different shades of one colour. He wanted people to **concentrate** on looking at the colours themselves, not what they were meant to be showing.

Follow the monkeys to the
Abstract Expressionist Gallery.
Can you see ...

A hanging monkey?

Colourful stripes?

A black mouth?

A curly tail?

Extra spots

A pair of **binoculars**

A **piece of watermelon**

A **party hat**

A **balloon**

A **spotty bow tie**

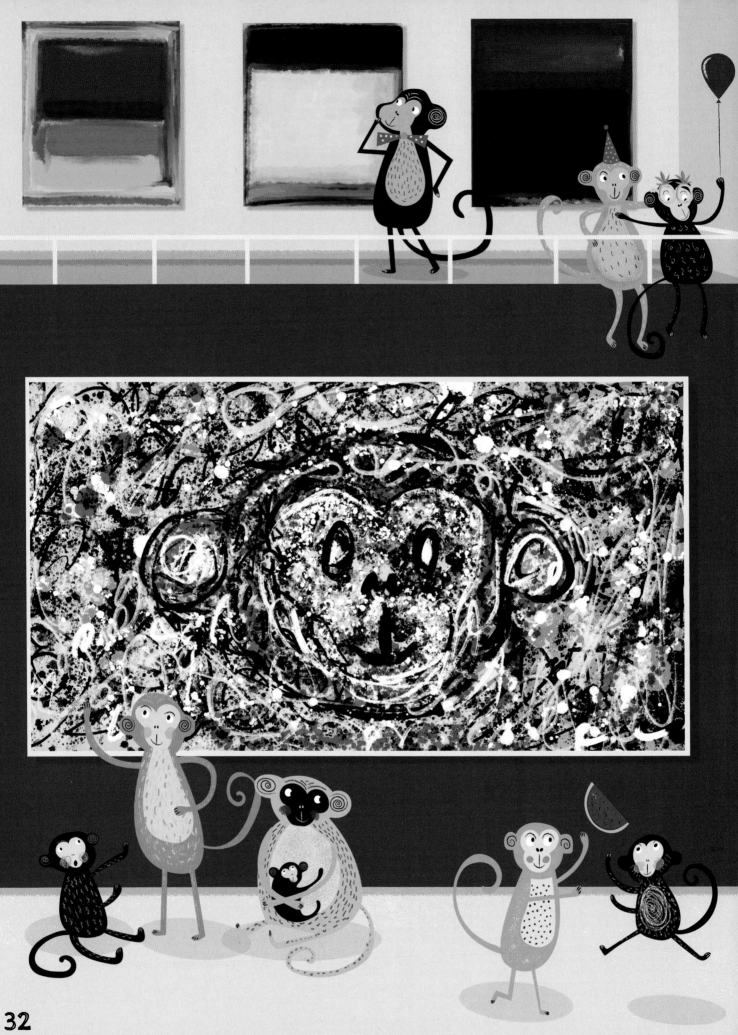

Adverts and Objects

The dogs are keen to read about POP ART. All the work looks very bright and colourful.

Pop Artists make art from items in **popular culture** that are all around us, such as **adverts**, **comic books** and **everyday products**. Andy Warhol, for example, painted pictures of soup cans.

The most famous Pop Artists were **Andy Warhol, Roy Lichtenstein** and **Keith Haring**.

Pop Artists gave people a **new idea** of what art could be – it was about the world they were living in and **everyone** could see parts of their lives in Pop Art creations.

Join the dogs as they go to the Pop Art Gallery. Can you spot ...

A green and red can?

SPANIEL'S SOUP

A rainbow flower?

A dog on a diving board?

Two teary eyes?

PUP ART

Extra spots

A baseball cap

A yellow collar

A pet tortoise

A ball

A black handbag

Pop Art Gallery

Tricks and Movement

The penguins are learning about OP ART. It all looks so strange – they can barely believe their eyes!

The most famous Op Artists include **Bridget Riley**, **Victor Vasarely** and **Jesús Rafael Soto**.

Op Art stands for '**Optical Art**'. Optical relates to our **sight**. These artists mix shapes, colours and patterns to trick our eyes. It often seems that images they've painted are **moving** around.

Op Artists were inspired by the work of the artist **M.C. Escher**. His work *Hand with Reflecting Sphere*, for example, showed an interest in tricks and illusion.

Follow the penguins to the
Op Art Gallery. Can you spot ...

An artist's studio?

A blue fish?

Three brown prints?

A white penguin?

Extra spots

An **ice-skating penguin**

A **fish flag**

A **woolly hat**

A **basket**

A pair of **earmuffs**

Op Art Gallery

FISH ART

Arty Animal Timeline

Impressionism
1860s
Edgar Degas
Claude Monet
Pierre-Auguste Renoir

Post-Impressionism
1880s
Paul Cézanne
Paul Gauguin
Vincent van Gogh
Georges Seurat

Op Art
1960s–1980s
Bridget Riley
Jesús Rafael Soto
Victor Vasarely

Pop Art
1950s–1970s
David Hockney
Keith Haring
Yayoi Kusama
Roy Lichtenstein
Takashi Murakami
Andy Warhol

This timeline shows the movements featured in the book and the main artists of each one.

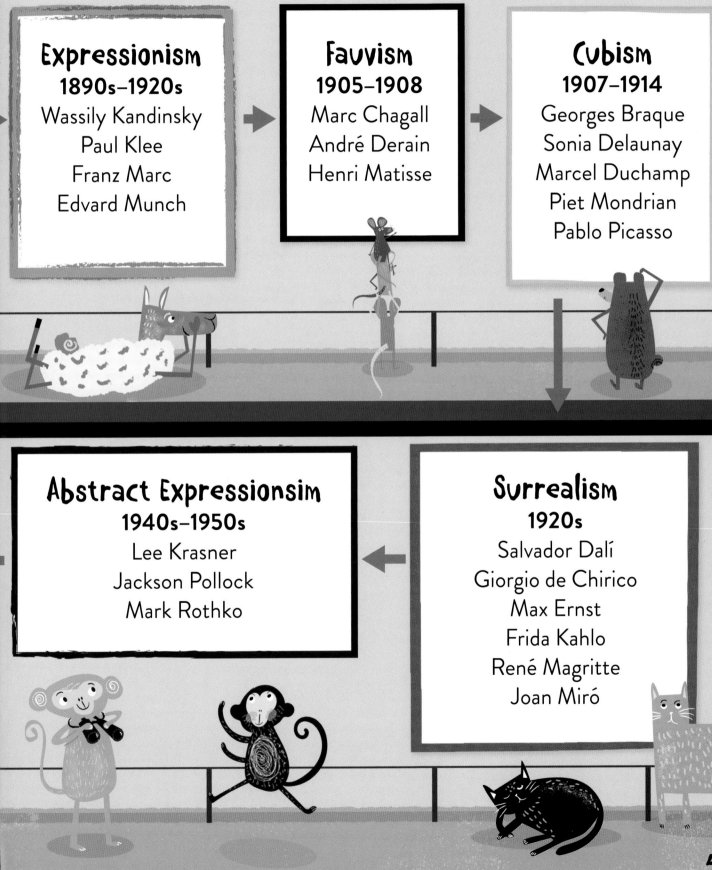

Expressionism
1890s–1920s
Wassily Kandinsky
Paul Klee
Franz Marc
Edvard Munch

Fauvism
1905–1908
Marc Chagall
André Derain
Henri Matisse

Cubism
1907–1914
Georges Braque
Sonia Delaunay
Marcel Duchamp
Piet Mondrian
Pablo Picasso

Abstract Expressionsim
1940s–1950s
Lee Krasner
Jackson Pollock
Mark Rothko

Surrealism
1920s
Salvador Dalí
Giorgio de Chirico
Max Ernst
Frida Kahlo
René Magritte
Joan Miró

Answers

Did you find everything?
Check your answers below.

p8–9: Impressionist Gallery

p12–13: Post-Impressionist Gallery

p16–17: Expressionist Gallery

p20–21: Fauvist Gallery

p24–25 Cubist Gallery

p28–29: Surrealist Gallery

p32–33: Abstract Expressionist Gallery

p36–37: Pop Art Gallery

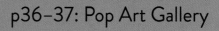

p40–41: Op Art Gallery

Arty Words

Abstract
In abstract art, things are presented in a way that is different from how they really appear.

Canvas
A canvas is the cloth surface that an artist paints on.

Collage
A collage is a picture that is made by sticking down different materials on a surface.

Emotion
An emotion is a feeling, such as love, fear, happiness or anger.

Geometric
Geometric refers to lines and shapes such as triangles, rectangles, squares and circles. Geometric art is art made out of these things.

Movement
An art movement is formed by a group of artists who have similar inspirations and ideas at a particular time.

Realistic
Realistic pictures are painted to produce an almost photographic image of an object.

Sculpture
A sculpture is a work of art made out of a solid material, such as wood or metal.